July 99

A GRANDPARENT'S
LITTLE INSTRUCTION BOOK

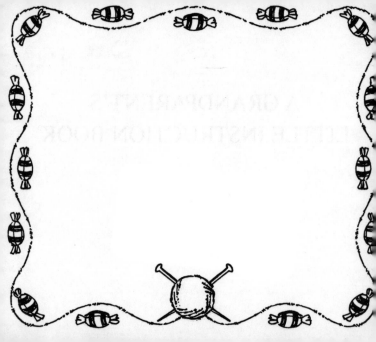

A GRANDPARENT'S
LITTLE INSTRUCTION BOOK

JASMINE BIRTLES

BOXTREE

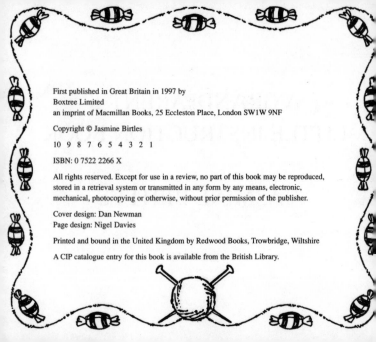

First published in Great Britain in 1997 by
Boxtree Limited
an imprint of Macmillan Books, 25 Eccleston Place, London SW1W 9NF

10 9 8 7 6 5 4 3 2 1

ISBN: 0 7522 2266 X

Cover design: Dan Newman
Page design: Nigel Davies

Printed and bound in the United Kingdom by Redwood Books, Trowbridge, Wiltshire

A CIP catalogue entry for this book is available from the British Library.

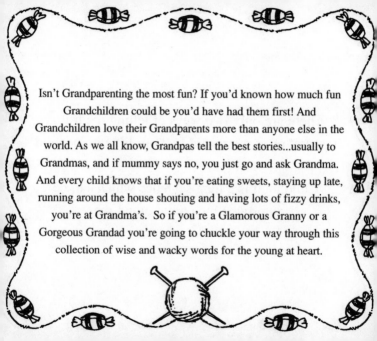

Isn't Grandparenting the most fun? If you'd known how much fun Grandchildren could be you'd have had them first! And Grandchildren love their Grandparents more than anyone else in the world. As we all know, Grandpas tell the best stories...usually to Grandmas, and if mummy says no, you just go and ask Grandma. And every child knows that if you're eating sweets, staying up late, running around the house shouting and having lots of fizzy drinks, you're at Grandma's. So if you're a Glamorous Granny or a Gorgeous Grandad you're going to chuckle your way through this collection of wise and wacky words for the young at heart.

There are only two ways of telling the truth:
in secret or as overheard by your little grandchild.

• • •

Childhood is a long sentence which can be
improved by a good grand-ma.

Grandparents can remember a time when they were so poor they couldn't afford poverty.

• • •

Don't worry if you don't get on with your children – that's what grandchildren are for.

You know you're a successful grandparent
when you emigrate and the family follows you.

• • •

It's ironic when your grandchildren
want to grow up like you – and you
aren't even aware that you grew up.

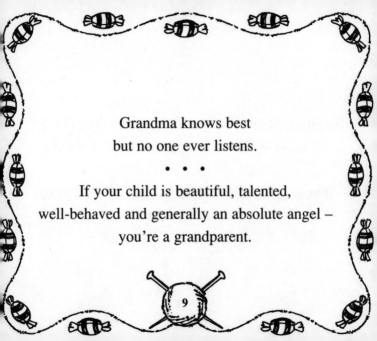

Grandma knows best
but no one ever listens.

• • •

If your child is beautiful, talented,
well-behaved and generally an absolute angel –
you're a grandparent.

9

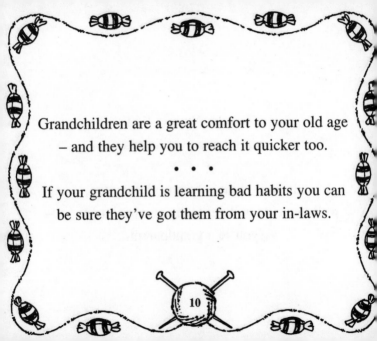

Grandchildren are a great comfort to your old age
– and they help you to reach it quicker too.

• • •

If your grandchild is learning bad habits you can
be sure they've got them from your in-laws.

10

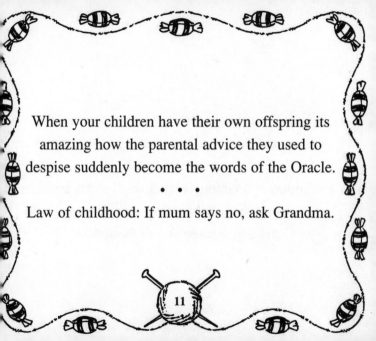

When your children have their own offspring its
amazing how the parental advice they used to
despise suddenly become the words of the Oracle.

• • •

Law of childhood: If mum says no, ask Grandma.

11

Grandparents know the score: they crochet, they quaver and they're always having to read notes.

• • •

Definition of a Granny Flat: a small room given in return for 24-hour babysitting, free domestic help and a guarantee of an inheritance.

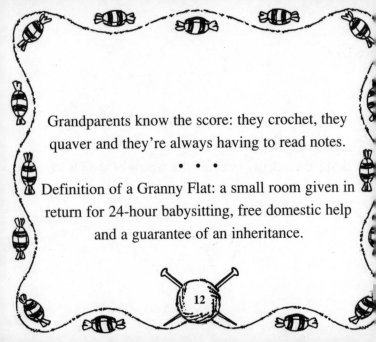

Grandchildren are living proof that
Nostalgia isn't what it used to be.

• • •

Don't bother telling your grandchildren about the
miles you walked to school and back each day.
Children nowadays only walk to the telly.

13

Grandchildren are a blessing in disguise –
especially at Halloween.

• • •

Grandmother's law: you put on a jumper
when I am cold, you eat when I am hungry
and you go to bed when I am tired.

The best thing about grandchildren is that they haven't heard your stories before.

• • •

You know you have well brought up grandchildren if they send you their Christmas thank-you notes before the next Christmas.

If you're looking for popular clothes
to buy your teenage granddaughter
just pick anything that is badly-made,
the colour of sick and no bigger
than an Elastoplast.

If the little grandchildren turn up
their noses at your homemade stew
remind them that it is special adults' stew
that children aren't allowed to have.
Guess what they'll insist on having for dinner?

Delightful grandchildren belong to the whole family. Rude children belong to a daughter-in-law.

• • •

Have you noticed how grandchildren never go around showing photos of their grandparents?

Enjoy old age – it's the one thing
you can do better than the youngsters.

• • •

Have a second childhood –
as many times as you can manage.

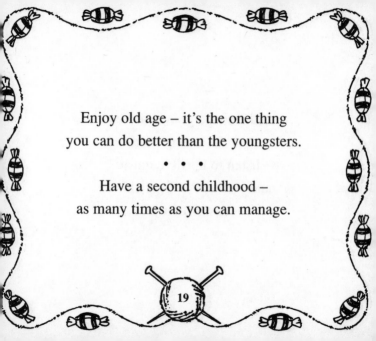

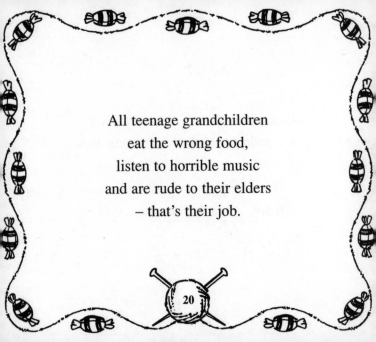

All teenage grandchildren
eat the wrong food,
listen to horrible music
and are rude to their elders
– that's their job.

When you've reached a certain age
the only things you're allowed to do
are things you don't enjoy, things you
never did before and things
you've already forgotten how to do.

Don't be ashamed of your age.
Tell people how old you are
on your birthday…
when it comes round
every five years.

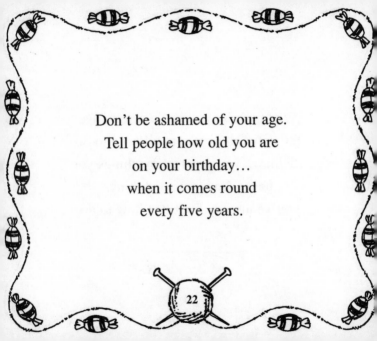

You know you're old
if you ask for a minute steak
in a restaurant and the waiter
asks for the money
up front.

You know you're really, *really* old
if your blood type is discontinued.

• • •

If a child offers you a seat on the bus,
check first for chewing gum.

Grandchildren are like waiters –
none of them will come when you call

• • •

Don't bother trying to stay healthy –
just find an ailment you enjoy.

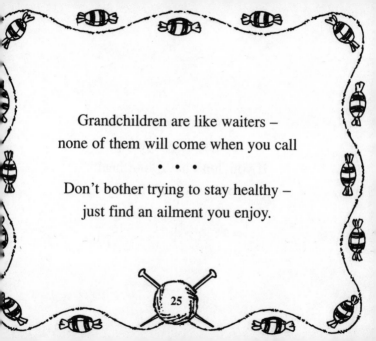

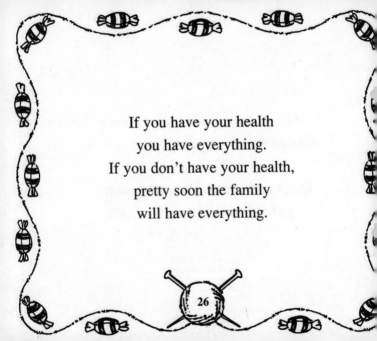

If you have your health
you have everything.
If you don't have your health,
pretty soon the family
will have everything.

26

The latest culinary style is
Cuisine Grandmere. Translated
that means anything that hasn't
been microwaved, bought in a packet
or delivered on a moped.

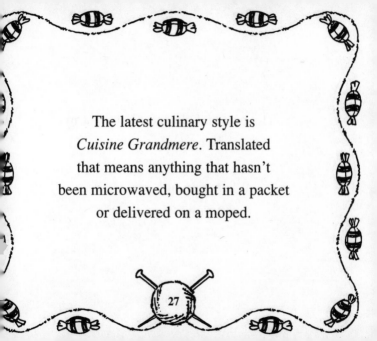

The best and cheapest baby alarm
is a grandparent.

• • •

When grandma gets tired,
everyone takes a nap.

Never miss a good opportunity
not to give advice.

• • •

Stop worrying about your health.
It'll go away.

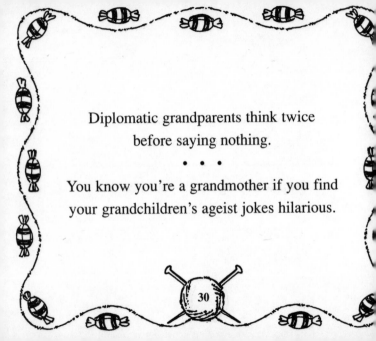

Diplomatic grandparents think twice
before saying nothing.

• • •

You know you're a grandmother if you find
your grandchildren's ageist jokes hilarious.

30

Granddads are made
for hugging.

• • •

Grandparents may have winter on their heads
but the joys of spring are always in their hearts.

If the children are eating sweets,
staying up late, running around
the house shouting and having
lots of fizzy drinks,
they're at Grandma's.

Grandparents have their
own brand of playfulness…
a particularly favourite game is to play
'Cutting our children out of our wills
if they don't let us visit soon'.

Grandparents are the foundation of the family –
they're real bricks.

• • •

Grandparents have practical wisdom.
Son-in-laws have practically no sense at all.

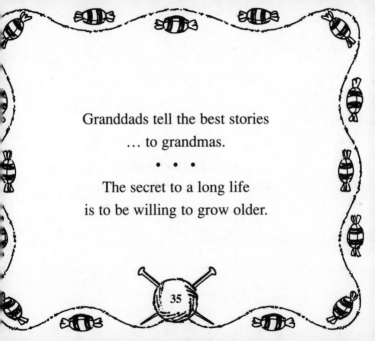

Granddads tell the best stories
… to grandmas.

• • •

The secret to a long life
is to be willing to grow older.

Grandparents have most
in common with
their grandchildren –
both have lots of things to hide
from mummy and daddy.

Being a grandparent means
that just when you thought
you were an ordinary person
you become 'Superperson' because
some little people think you are.

Grandchildren need training
but sadly grandparents aren't allowed
to be team coach – they have to sit
at the sidelines and allow
less competent people do the job.

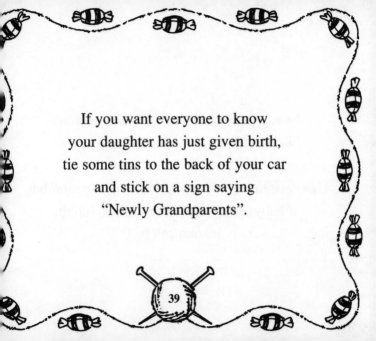

If you want everyone to know
your daughter has just given birth,
tie some tins to the back of your car
and stick on a sign saying
"Newly Grandparents".

As any grandchild knows, varicose veins
make a fantastic racetrack for toy cars.

• • •

Grandparenting is not a full-time occupation but,
if babysitting rates in the area are high,
it soon can be.

Grandchildren are such fun
you should have had them first.

• • •

A grandchild is a little person who
likes your food better than their mum's.

Take a tip from Father Christmas –
visit once a year.

• • •

Thank goodness for the 'baby-boom' –
it's created an even bigger 'grandma-boom'.

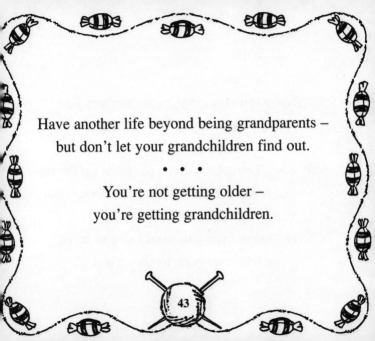

Have another life beyond being grandparents –
but don't let your grandchildren find out.

• • •

You're not getting older –
you're getting grandchildren.

43

You're old enough to be a grandma if:
...young people say "I hope I'm like you
when I'm your age."
...people with crutches offer you a seat on the bus.
...no one looks surprised when you show your
pensioner's discount card.
...the fitness instructor looks at you when
she tells everyone to take a rest.

44

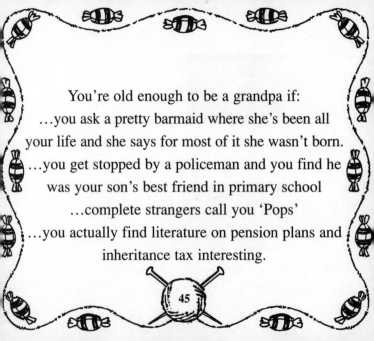

You're old enough to be a grandpa if:

…you ask a pretty barmaid where she's been all your life and she says for most of it she wasn't born.

…you get stopped by a policeman and you find he was your son's best friend in primary school

…complete strangers call you 'Pops'

…you actually find literature on pension plans and inheritance tax interesting.

45

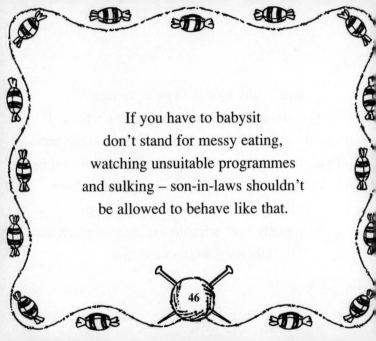

If you have to babysit
don't stand for messy eating,
watching unsuitable programmes
and sulking – son-in-laws shouldn't
be allowed to behave like that.

Remember when naughty children were spanked? Now their 'anti-social behaviour stemming from suppressed anger against parental control' has to be monitored by a child psychologist.

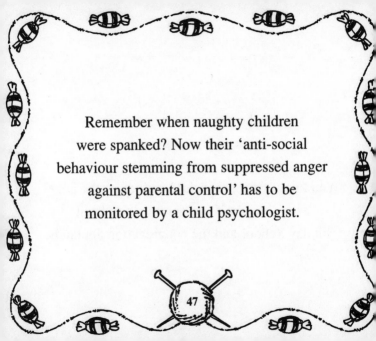

By the time you're grown up
you're growing down.

• • •

You know your grandchild isn't quite the angel
you thought if you remove him from
Sunday School and the congregation applauds.

You'll never feel the cold
if your grandma likes to knit.

• • •

Children used to take turns washing and
drying the dishes. Now they just get a go
at pressing the dishwasher button.

Children used to be told
to get home in time for tea.
Now you have to ring
their mobiles to make
an appointment.

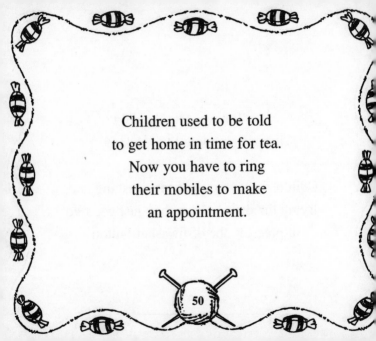

Remember when you told the children
to look both ways before
crossing the road? Now they won't go
outside the house unless they're
on something already on wheels.

If you have to look after
your baby grandchild
make sure his nappy is loose –
they move more slowly
that way.

You know you have a
problem grandchild if you never
have pictures to stick on the
fridge door – they're all drawn
just above the skirting board.

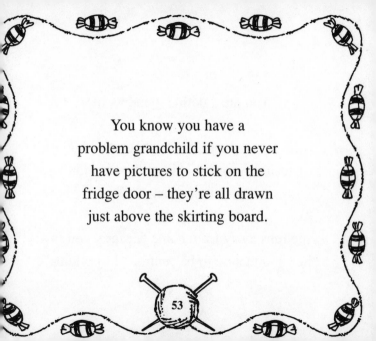

You are a doting grandma if:

…he terrorises all the neighbourhood dogs because, you say, "his mother wouldn't give him a hamster."

…he runs away from home because, you say, "he's too mature to be controlled by adults."

…he's caught cheating at school, which means that "the teachers just can't accept that he's a genius – they have to find some excuse for his good marks."

…he gets stopped for speeding "because the speed limit is ridiculously low."

If you have run out of people
to show your grandchildren's photos to,
pretend you have lost your
senior citizen's card on the bus and
show the conductor their photos as
proof of your age.

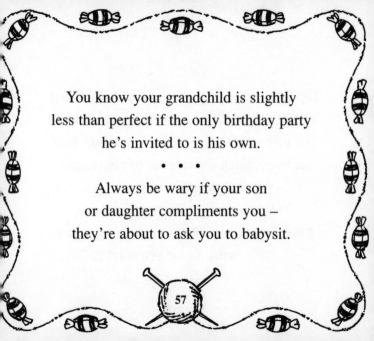

You know your grandchild is slightly
less than perfect if the only birthday party
he's invited to is his own.

• • •

Always be wary if your son
or daughter compliments you –
they're about to ask you to babysit.

57

Top three ways of getting out of babysitting:
1) Tell your offspring you'd love to babysit
because you were planning on telling your
grandchildren the facts of life next time
you had them for an evening.
2) When you get the phonecall say,
"Just a moment, I have to cough up again
...now, what was it you wanted?"

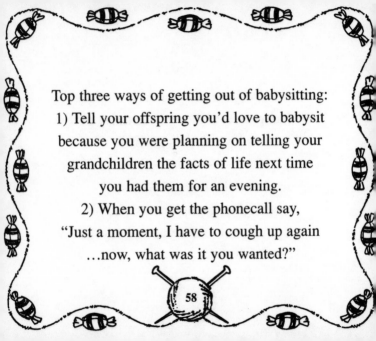

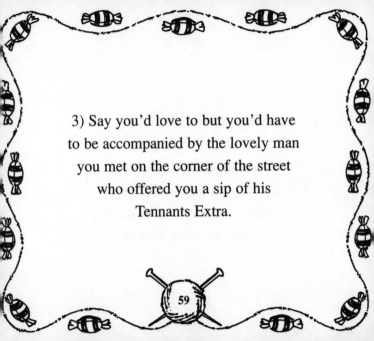

3) Say you'd love to but you'd have to be accompanied by the lovely man you met on the corner of the street who offered you a sip of his Tennants Extra.

If you're having trouble
losing weight wear your
bathing costume in front
of your grandchildren.
Their comments will soon give
your diet fresh impetus.

60

Things you'll never hear a grandchild say:
1) I'm going to bed early.
2) I'd much rather watch soaps than cartoons.
3) Modern music is so boring, I'd much rather listen to Cole Porter.
4) Don't mind me, I'll just quietly read a book in the corner.
5) Oh I don't mind if you've bought me something or not, I'm just happy to see you.

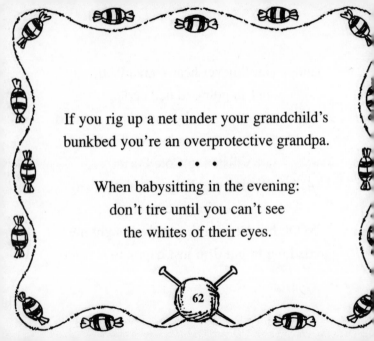

If you rig up a net under your grandchild's
bunkbed you're an overprotective grandpa.

• • •

When babysitting in the evening:
don't tire until you can't see
the whites of their eyes.

62

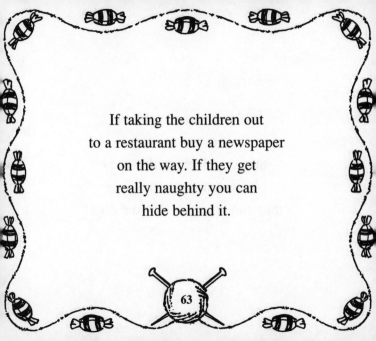

If taking the children out
to a restaurant buy a newspaper
on the way. If they get
really naughty you can
hide behind it.

63

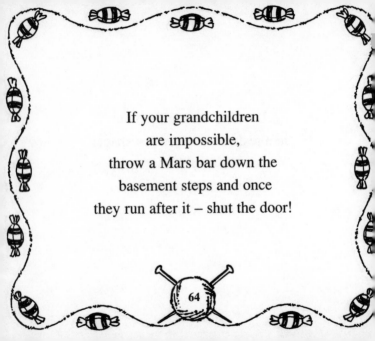

If your grandchildren
are impossible,
throw a Mars bar down the
basement steps and once
they run after it – shut the door!

64

The shortest space of time
in life is the period between
your children being old enough
not to wreck your furniture and
your grandchildren starting.

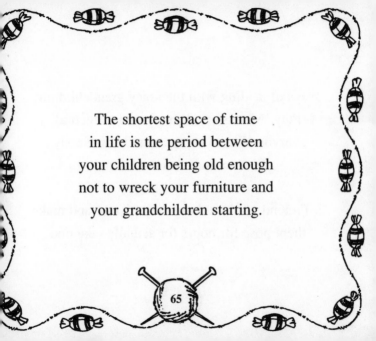

Ways of dealing with the noisy grandchildren:
1. Play 'Monastery, Library and Cathedral' –
   everyone has to creep around noiselessly.
   First to make a sound is out.

2. Pretend you're taking their picture and make
   them pose for hours (or actually take one

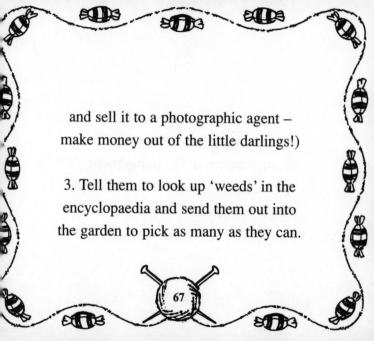

and sell it to a photographic agent –
make money out of the little darlings!)

3. Tell them to look up 'weeds' in the
encyclopaedia and send them out into
the garden to pick as many as they can.

67

Children use any excuse
to get out of bed. After the ninth
appearance in the living room
you'll begin to hope that the sound
of footsteps is a burglar.

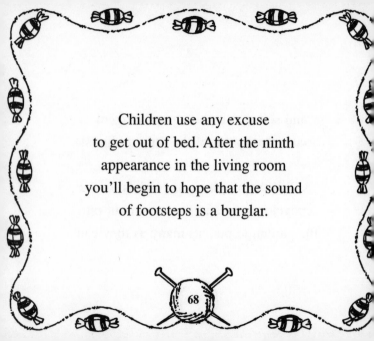

When your grandchildren
are born insist they
get godparents, after all,
someone's got to share the
babysitting duties.

Never try voice lessons. Your children still won't listen to your grandparental advice.

• • •

Grandmas can't get away with telling children to "do that or else!" Her "or else" usually means forgiveness.

You can't buy love but your grandchildren
will be disappointed if you don't try.

• • •

You're an overprotective grandma if
you buy your grandchildren fluorescent pyjamas
in case they sleepwalk.

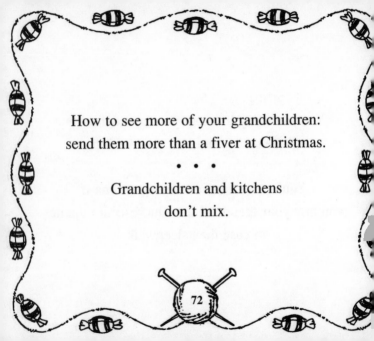

How to see more of your grandchildren:
send them more than a fiver at Christmas.

• • •

Grandchildren and kitchens
don't mix.

72

Grandmas know that all a difficult child needs is a little 'yessing' in a world of 'no's'.

• • •

When taking the grandchildren out to eat pick somewhere noisy. It'll drown them out.

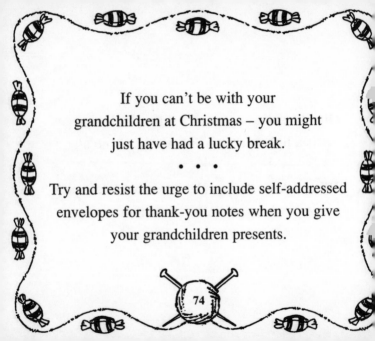

If you can't be with your
grandchildren at Christmas – you might
just have had a lucky break.

• • •

Try and resist the urge to include self-addressed
envelopes for thank-you notes when you give
your grandchildren presents.

74

You have to really love your grandchildren
to take them to a funfair.

• • •

Telling your grandchildren the real meaning of
Christmas won't stop them wailing when they
don't get the toy they want.

On long journeys, kids get carsick and
grandparents get kidsick.

• • •

It's best to stop kissing your grandchildren's
cuts when they start shaving.

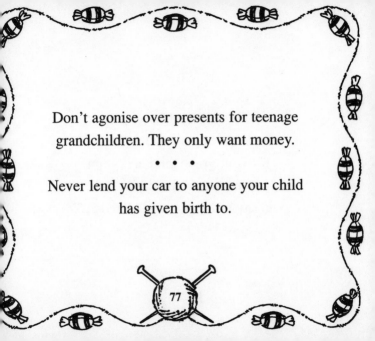

Don't agonise over presents for teenage grandchildren. They only want money.

• • •

Never lend your car to anyone your child has given birth to.

77

You can remortgage your
house to buy a special present
for your grandchild and mum
will still have to remind him "what do
you say to Granny and Grandpa?"

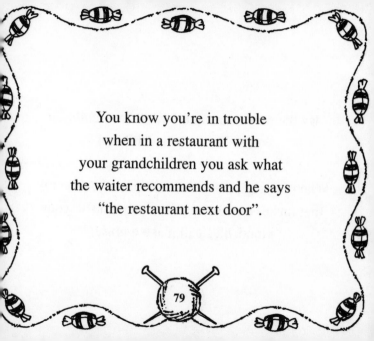

You know you're in trouble
when in a restaurant with
your grandchildren you ask what
the waiter recommends and he says
"the restaurant next door".

By the time you can afford to have children you're having grandchildren.

• • •

When buying presents remember, when the toy that makes a noise stops making a noise your grandchild will make a noise.

Never hit your grandchildren.
They may be armed.

• • •

If you want to buy a present for your grandchild
that will be popular, ignore anything their
mother suggests.

When your grandchild reaches up
to hold your hand it's usually to lead you
down to the toy department.

• • •

Today, grandmas aren't hot from baking, they're
hot from dancing and boogying all night.

Don't let your grandchild drive you until
you're sure she not only knows right from
wrong but right from left.

• • •

Grandchild's law: Grandpa's is not to reason why,
Grandpa's is but to buy and buy.

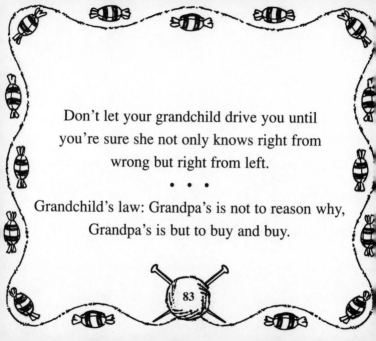

You may not be ready to be grandparents
if you have a personalised license plate
which reads KDSRGON.

• • •

Do you have a social life or are the
grandchildren still at home?

84

Grandmas aren't just for babysitting, they're also for babywalking, baby-feeding, baby-dressing, babyminding, baby-talking…

• • •

Grandpas are fun to kiss because their whiskers are softer than dad's.

Grandparents always listen to what
their grandchildren have to say.
They're looking for ideas.

• • •

A parent passes on biology,
a grandparent, history.

You are not ready to be called 'Grandma' if:

1) You're pregnant with a child of your own.

2) You look, sound and dance like Tina Turner.

3) You've been asked to model for Wonderbra.

4) Mel Gibson called you up last time he was in town.

5) You just don't feel like it.

Teenagers get on with
grandparents better than
with their parents – they both
understand the importance
of sleeping.

Grandma knows that the
three most important things in life
are saying your prayers, loving
your family and friends and never
missing a sale at Woolies.

Grandparents and grandchildren get on so well because they have a common enemy – parents.

• • •

Grandpas are good at showing you the family tree – and pointing out the dead wood on your grandma's side.

A grandparent is both a bouncy castle
and a crumbling ruin.

• • •

If you can't get the grandchildren to go to bed,
entice them with promises of embarrassing stories
about what their dad did when he was their age.

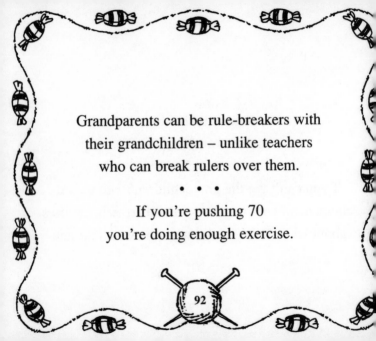

Grandparents can be rule-breakers with
their grandchildren – unlike teachers
who can break rulers over them.

• • •

If you're pushing 70
you're doing enough exercise.

92

A father never knew it could be so difficult
to raise a child. A grandfather never knew
it could be so easy.

• • •

If you can't afford a facelift,
have your body lowered.

All parents are amateurs,
it's grandparents who are the professionals.

• • •

Grandparents are popular with children because
they have time on their hands – parents usually
have rubber gloves on theirs.

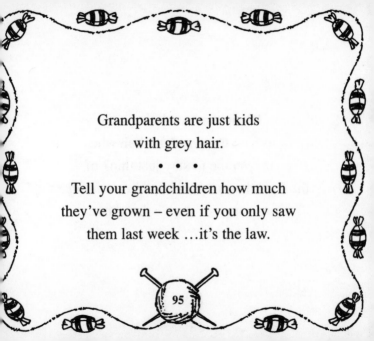

Grandparents are just kids
with grey hair.

• • •

Tell your grandchildren how much
they've grown – even if you only saw
them last week …it's the law.

95

If you are wondering what
to feed the grandchildren when
they come to stay just think of
the food their mother wouldn't want them
to have – and give them that.

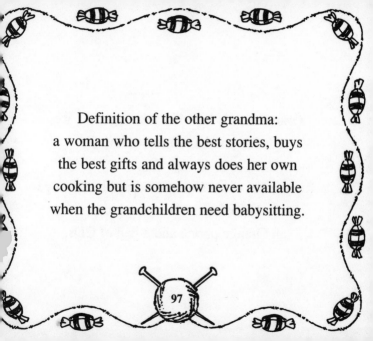

Definition of the other grandma:
a woman who tells the best stories, buys
the best gifts and always does her own
cooking but is somehow never available
when the grandchildren need babysitting.

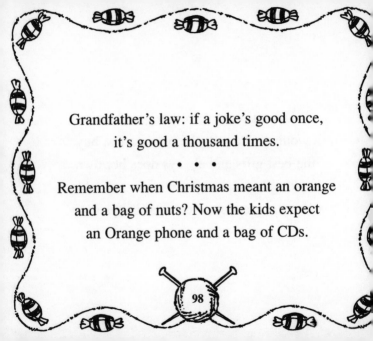

Grandfather's law: if a joke's good once,
it's good a thousand times.

• • •

Remember when Christmas meant an orange
and a bag of nuts? Now the kids expect
an Orange phone and a bag of CDs.

98

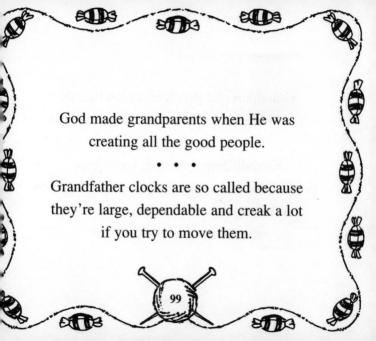

God made grandparents when He was creating all the good people.

• • •

Grandfather clocks are so called because they're large, dependable and creak a lot if you try to move them.

99

Grandparental joy: finding out that the grandchildren prefer *your* computer game.

• • •

Grandparental misery: buying the grandchildren a computer game for Christmas and finding the *other* grandparents bought them a more expensive one.

Grandmas are famous for
their sayings like
"Beauty is only skin deep",
"Ladies don't sweat, they glow"
and "No, I can't lend you a fiver,
go and ask your mother".

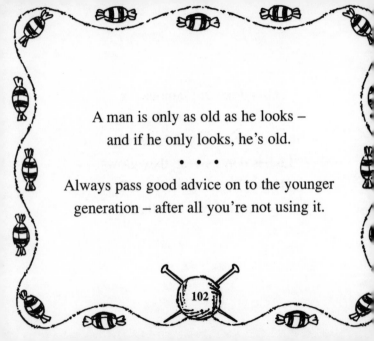

A man is only as old as he looks –
and if he only looks, he's old.

• • •

Always pass good advice on to the younger
generation – after all you're not using it.

102

A child's view of grandma's house:
the sweet shop that's always open.

• • •

Grandchildren are the best excuse
you'll ever get for a second childhood.

Grandchildren are handy for getting at those hard-to-reach places, like your shoelaces.

• • •

Grandchildren can help you keep fit. When they're little they exercise your patience; when they're teenagers they exercise your imagination.

You're a grandma when you become the
joke you didn't understand.

• • •

When you're a first-time grandma you suddenly
realise how much you've forgotten about babies –
like which end produces liquid first.

Absent-minded is losing your glasses.
Carelessness is losing the grandchildren.

• • •

Grandfathers do it later.

• • •

Don't bother having children –
only have grandchildren.

Grandmas always give the best advice
on babycare – "Ask the health visitor."

• • •

You've been married too long if your wife
tells you you're only interested in one thing –
and you can't remember what it is.

Having grandchildren means being
able to eat ice-cream without guilt.

• • •

You're getting on when what your grandchildren
study as history is what you used to study as
current affairs.

Things grandmothers look forward to:
1) French designers deciding that Dr Scholl sandals are the 'in' look.
2) Being chosen as Jamie Lee Curtis's body-double.
3) *Not* being chosen as Elizabeth Taylor's body-double.

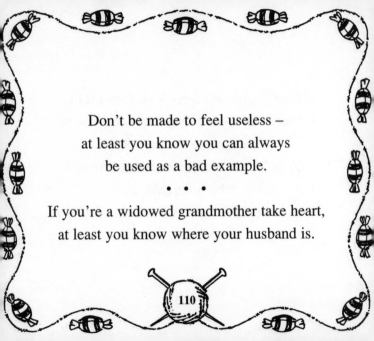

Don't be made to feel useless –
at least you know you can always
be used as a bad example.

• • •

If you're a widowed grandmother take heart,
at least you know where your husband is.

The worst thing about growing old for a man
is he has to sleep with a grandmother.

• • •

The worst thing about growing old for a woman
is *she* has to sleep with a grandfather.

With all this sleeping around children
should start lecturing their grandparents.

• • •

You know you're old fashioned if you can't
send your grandchildren letters because
your quill's broken.

You know you're old if the picture
on your passport is by Holbein.

• • •

Just imagine how proud Grandma Moses
was of her son. How many other grandchildren
could part an entire sea?

You know you're getting on a bit when you sit on a rocking chair and you can't get it started.

• • •

Child's view: A grandma is a nice lady who stops your parents shouting at you.

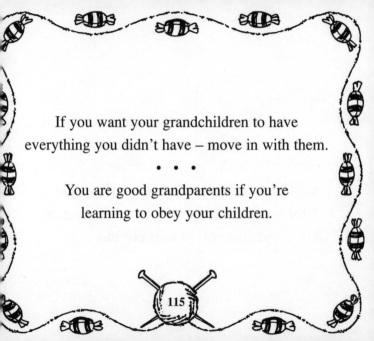

If you want your grandchildren to have
everything you didn't have – move in with them.

• • •

You are good grandparents if you're
learning to obey your children.

115

You're getting on if all you want for your birthday is not to be reminded of it.

• • •

Here's a quick cure if you start to pine for your grandchildren – go to a restaurant and sit next to someone else's.

Once you're a grandfather, a hair in
the head is worth two in the brush.

• • •

You know you're getting absentminded if
you can never find your glasses –
you just leave them where you emptied them.

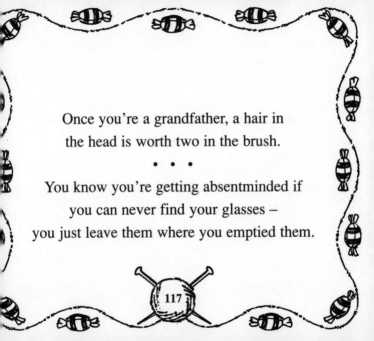

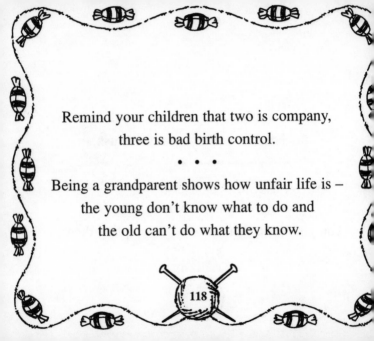

Remind your children that two is company,
three is bad birth control.

• • •

Being a grandparent shows how unfair life is –
the young don't know what to do and
the old can't do what they know.

118

People are staying younger for
so much longer it takes at least 20 years
to get used to how old you are.

• • •

If you're short-sighted there's an easy way
to find your grandchild when you're babysitting –
don't change his nappies.

Have fun when you're babysitting in the evening.
Phone your children and ask where
they keep the fire extinguisher.

• • •

Show me a woman who does what she wants
and I'll show you a grandma on her own.

You're getting on if the candles on
your birthday cake set off the smoke alarm.

• • •

Definition of a bore: someone who goes on
and on about their grandchildren when all you
want to talk about it yours.

You know you're getting on if
your favourite card game is 'dress' poker.

• • •

Confuse your family.
Name yourself as beneficiary in your will.

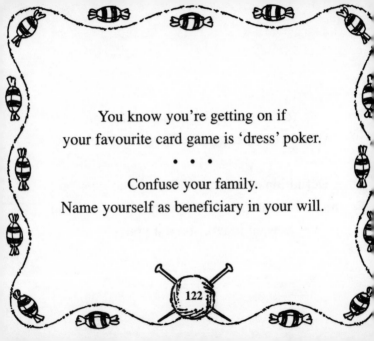

Teach your grandchild the value of money.
Remortgage her dollshouse.

• • •

A glamorous grandmother is one who
wears black suspenders, in memory of
those who passed beyond.

If you think your family couldn't care
if you were alive or dead, try missing a few
birthdays and Christmas's.

• • •

When you're in your car be careful of children,
they're terrible drivers.

Experience is what you have
when you're too old to get a job.

• • •

How is it that the man who wasn't good enough
to marry your daughter is now the father of the
most wonderful children in the world?

Of course it was better in your day…
if you can remember when your day was.

• • •

Every father was a child once and every
grandmother thinks he still is.

You're a grandad if gorgeous women
don't bother you – and you wish they would.

• • •

When your children ask you if they're bringing
up their children well, honesty is the best policy.
Keeping your mouth shut is even better.

Jasmine Birtles has appeared on literally hundreds of TV programmes – in the audience. Her favourite role is being the 'third woman from the right in the second row'. A nonconformist in family matters she has put off having children but is waiting for the right man with whom to have grandchildren. She is the editor of several books aimed at Grandparents including *Pride and Prejudice: An Anatomy of the Daughter-in-law* and *War and Peace: Christmas With the Family*.